# AN INTRODUCTION TO GENETICS

## FOR KIDS

### WRITTEN AND ILLUSTRATED BY
# JANE ZEBRACK

**Shriners Hospitals**
for Children™
**Love to the rescue.®**

All of the profits from this book are donated to the
Shriners Hospitals for Children®

ISBN: 978-1-7328880-0-5

# TABLE OF CONTENTS

# GENES

**Genes** are like an instruction manual. They give the instructions for the development, growth, function, and reproduction of all living organisms. Genes are sequences that carry information about who we are and what makes each of us unique. They determine our **traits**, or characteristics, such as eye color and height. Every person has a set of genes, but the differences in traits between all of us come from small variations in our genes. Traits are often **inherited**, meaning that they are passed down from one generation to the next. You have similar characteristics as your parents because you inherit your genes from them. **Genetics**, the study of genes, is important because the understanding of how genes work helps scientists create new advancements with the potential to better society.

What traits have you inherited from your parents?

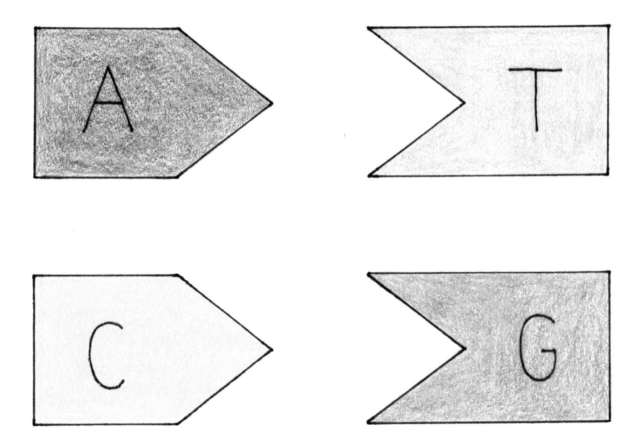

**DNA**, or deoxyribonucleic acid, contains genes. Its shape is a double helix, meaning that it is ladder-shaped and curves in a spiral. Each rung on the ladder has a set of two connecting bases. The four bases are adenine, thymine, cytosine, and guanine. Adenine always pairs with thymine, and cytosine always pairs with guanine. These bases are often abbreviated as a single letter: A, T, C, and G.

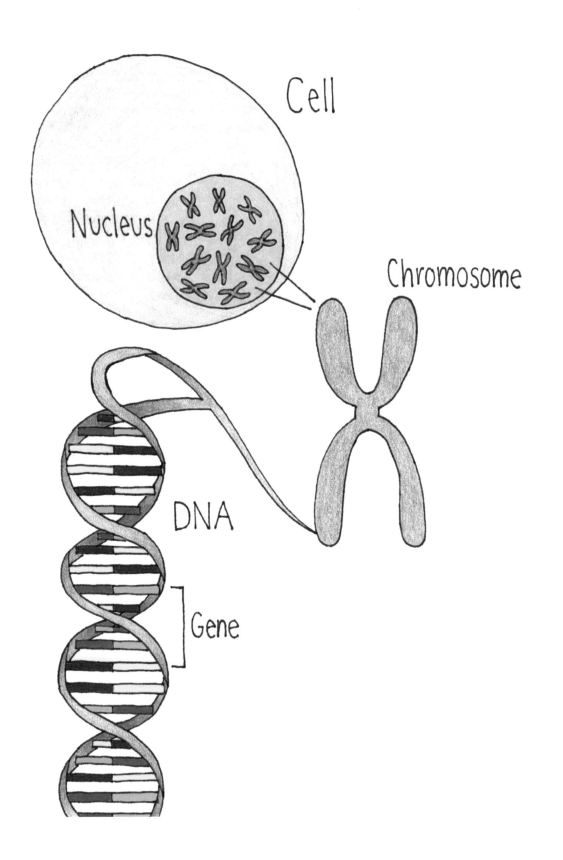

Cell

Nucleus

Chromosome

DNA

Gene

# CHROMOSOMES

DNA is organized into structures called chromosomes. Chromosomes are located in the nucleus of the cell. The cell is the basic unit of life of all organisms. The nucleus is a round organelle in the cell enclosed by a membrane.

Different species have a different number of chromosomes in each cell. Humans have 23 pairs of chromosomes for a total of 46 chromosomes. The 23rd pair determines your gender. Females have two copies of the X chromosome, and males have one copy of the X chromosome and one copy of the Y chromosome. A karyotype is a diagram that shows the number and appearance of the chromosomes in the nucleus of a cell.

To better understand the relationship between all of these structures, think of the cell as a cubby and the nucleus as a backpack inside the cubby. In the backpack, there are 46 textbooks, which are the chromosomes. The pages inside the textbooks are the DNA, and the words on those pages are the genes.

# MENDELIAN INHERITANCE

Originally, most people thought that inheritance was simply based on a blend of each parent's traits, like if you were to breed a white rose with a red rose and produce a pink rose. However, in the 1860s, Gregor Mendel developed a new theory of inheritance, Mendelian inheritance, through his observations of pea plants.

Mendel bred pea plants with purple flowers and pea plants with white flowers. The first generation of offspring (F1) only consisted of pea plants with purple flowers. However, in the second generation of offspring (F2), 75% of the offspring had purple flowers, and 25% of the offspring had white flowers.

So, how is this possible?

Different traits are determined by alleles, different forms of a single gene or trait. Each offspring has two alleles — one from each parent. Alleles always have one dominant form (A) and one recessive form (a). When an offspring has at least one dominant allele, it masks the presence of the recessive allele. The recessive trait will be present only if both alleles are recessive.

The F1 pea plants were all heterozygous, meaning that they had one dominant allele and one recessive allele (Aa). Thus, the F1 offspring exhibited the dominant trait, which is purple flowers.

The F2 pea plants contained a mixture of heterozygous and homozygous traits. The heterozygous plants had both dominant and recessive alleles (Aa), but only exhibited the dominant one, which is purple flowers. The plants that were homozygous had two of the same alleles, either both dominant (AA) or both recessive (aa). AA plants exhibited purple flowers, and aa plants exhibited white flowers.

An organism's genotype is the set of alleles that it carries. An organism's phenotype is its physical observable trait. A Punnett square is a square diagram used

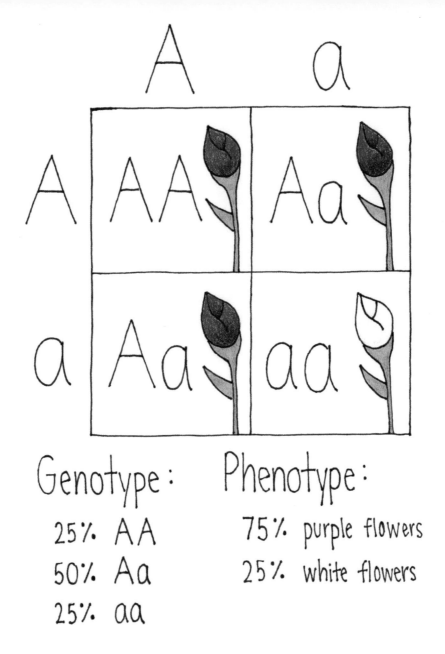

Genotype:
25% AA
50% Aa
25% aa

Phenotype:
75% purple flowers
25% white flowers

to predict the probability of offspring genotypes when breeding two organisms. If we looked at a Punnett square of two F1 pea plants from Mendel's experiment, the genotypes for flower color could be AA, Aa, or aa. The phenotypes would be purple for AA and Aa and white for aa. In terms of genotype, there would be a 50% likelihood of producing Aa and a 25% likelihood of producing either AA or aa. In terms of phenotype, there would be a 75% likelihood of producing a plant with purple flowers and a 25% likelihood of producing a plant with white flowers.

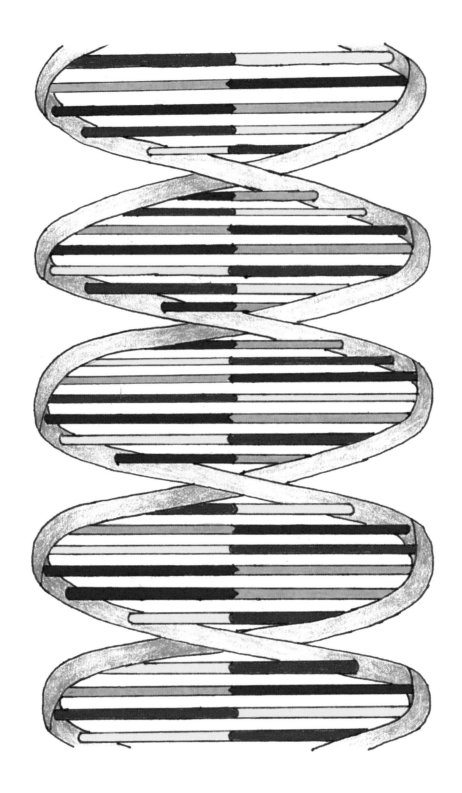

# THE HUMAN GENOME

A genome is the entire genetic code of an organism, which in humans is over 20,000 genes. The **Human Genome Project** was an international effort from 1990 to 2003 to discover the exact makeup of the genetic material of human beings. During the Human Genome Project, researchers deciphered the human genome by determining the order of all of the bases in our DNA. The Human Genome Project has given the world detailed information about the structure, organization, and function of the human genome.

# Original

```
T A C A G C T C A T T C
A T G T C G A G T A A G
```

# Substitution

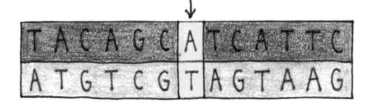

```
T A C A G | A | T C A T T C
A T G T C | T | A G T A A G
```

# Insertion

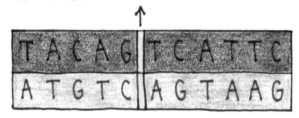

```
T A C A G C | A | T C A T T C
A T G T C G | T | A G T A A G
```

# Deletion

```
T A C A G | T C A T T C
A T G T C | A G T A A G
```

# MUTATIONS

A **mutation** is a change in the sequence of an organism's DNA. There are three main types of mutations: **substitutions**, **insertions**, and **deletions**. In a substitution mutation, the original base is replaced by a different base, such as from C to A. Insertions occur when an extra base is inserted into the gene sequence, and deletions occur when a base is taken out of the gene sequence.

Mutations cause genetic variation, which in turn produces genetic diversity among species. Genetic diversity is important because it results in **evolution**, the process of the gradual changes of traits that take place over many generations. When a mutation occurs that is beneficial to the survival and reproduction of the organism, the new genetic variant continues through reproduction and becomes more abundant over time. Eventually, the population with the mutation may become different from the original population that lacked the mutation.

# Down Syndrome Karyotype

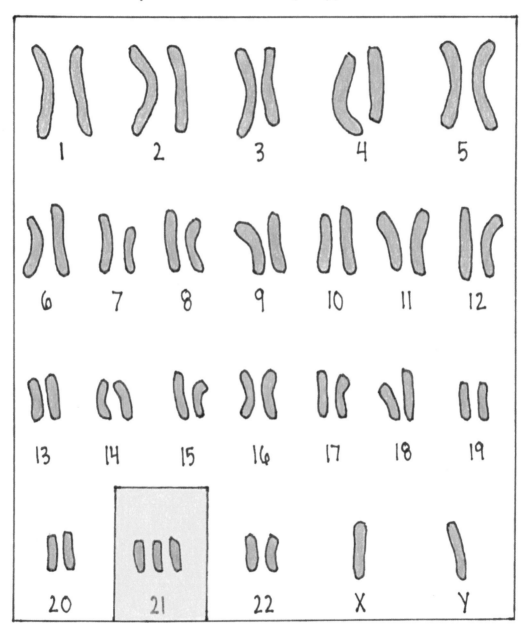

# GENETIC DISORDERS

Genetic disorders are conditions produced by an abnormality in DNA, such as a change in a chromosome or a mutation in a single gene.

Down Syndrome, also known as trisomy 21, occurs when there are three copies of the twenty-first chromosome instead of two. Characteristics include distinct facial features, intellectual disabilities, and a variety of health conditions, such as heart, hearing, and vision problems.

Duchenne Muscular Dystrophy is a muscle weakness disorder that occurs from a mutation of a gene on the X chromosome (X-linked disorder). This mutation causes a lack of dystrophin, a protein that keeps muscles strong. Duchenne Muscular Dystrophy usually affects males because they have only one X chromosome. Since females have two X chromosomes, a mutation would have to occur at both genes on both X chromosomes for them to have the disorder. A Y-linked disorder is caused by a gene mutation located on the Y chromosome. It would be passed on only from father to son because only males have a Y chromosome.

Sickle cell disease is one of the most common genetic disorders in the world. It is caused by a mutation in the hemoglobin-Beta gene found on chromosome 11. This disease results in abnormal hemoglobin in red blood cells, making the cells distorted or "sickled." Sickle cell disease can cause anemia, infections, severe pain, and organ damage.

Cystic fibrosis is a genetic disorder that is caused by a genetic mutation of the cystic fibrosis transmembrane conductance regulator (CFTR) protein. This gene is on chromosome 7. When the CFTR protein is not working correctly, mucus and digestive liquids become thick and plug up airways and intestines. Symptoms include cough, breathing difficulties, and digestive problems.

Both sickle cell disease and cystic fibrosis are autosomal recessive disorders. In an autosomal recessive disorder, two copies of an abnormal gene, one from each parent, must be present in order for the disease to develop. Parents who have one normal gene and one abnormal gene that could be passed on to their children are called carriers.

In autosomal dominant disorders, only one abnormal gene from one parent is needed to acquire the disease. An example of an autosomal dominant disorder is Marfan Syndrome, caused by a genetic mutation on chromosome 15 that results in abnormal connective tissue throughout the body.

Do you know anyone with a genetic disorder?

# NORMAL    SICKLE CELL

DNA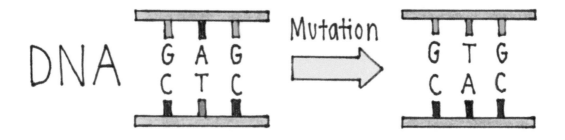

RED BLOOD CELL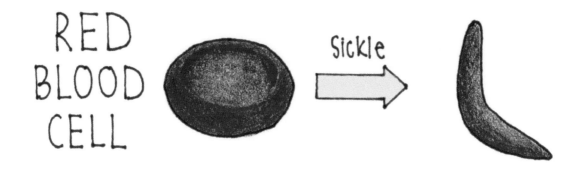

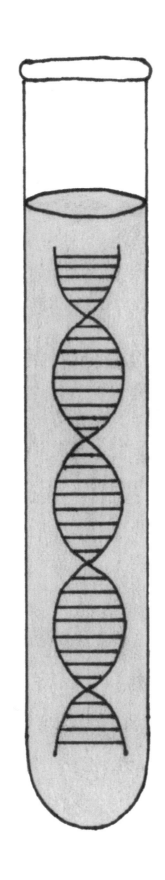

# GENE TESTING

The study of genetics has led to the innovative technology of **gene testing**. Gene testing can be used by doctors to diagnosis genetic disorders or to predict one's risk for a disease. Testing is available for thousands of genetic conditions and is typically performed on samples of saliva or blood. The DNA is extracted from the sample to examine the genetic material.

Companies also sell home DNA test kits that give you information about your genes, such as your **ancestry** and whether or not you have a certain mutation. Ancestry is a person's ethnic origin or descent (where one's ancestors came from). These tests compare your DNA to someone that is 100% of a certain ancestry to see how similar your DNA is to theirs. They also look at specific genes that would suggest a mutation to conclude whether or not you have the mutation.

Gene testing can give people knowledge about themselves that they otherwise may not have known. It can be very helpful if it gives them information related to their health and tells them if they are susceptible to a certain disease.

Have you ever wondered where your ancestors came from?

# GENETIC COUNSELING

**Genetic counseling** can help people understand their own risk and their family's risks for genetic diseases. Genetic counseling is done by a genetic counselor who has had specialized education and training in genetics. Genetic counselors ask about family history and educate patients and families. They can also help patients better understand the psychological aspects of genetic testing, recommend genetic tests if indicated, and interpret test results. For example, a husband and wife who have a family history of cystic fibrosis may decide to see a genetic counselor and discuss genetic testing to see if they carry the abnormal gene. Furthermore, a woman with several female relatives with breast cancer may discuss with a genetic counselor the pros and cons of being tested for the breast cancer gene, BRCA.

# GMO

# NON-GMO

# GENETIC ENGINEERING

**Genetic engineering**, or genetic modification, is a technology that is used to change the genetic makeup of an organism. Plants, animals, or microorganisms that have had their DNA changed through genetic engineering are called **genetically modified organisms** (GMOs).

Genetic engineering has been used in agriculture and medicine. Certain types of crops, such as corn and soybeans, have been genetically modified to prevent diseases and create more nutritious food. Although scientists have proven that GMO foods do not pose a greater health risk than non-GMO foods, many people still have concerns that they are not as safe. Genetic engineering has also been used to create many important medications and hormones for the treatment of diseases. For example, genetic engineering was used to modify bacteria's DNA to enable the production of human insulin, a hormone used to treat diabetes.

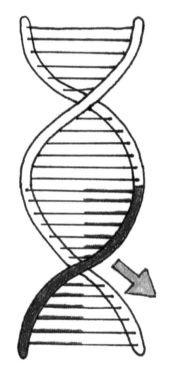
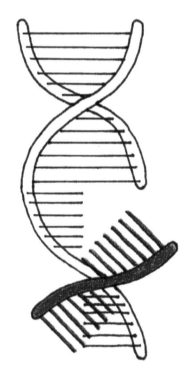
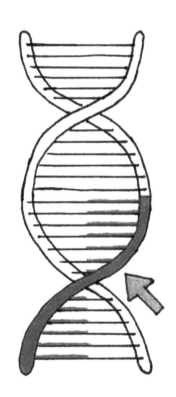

# GENE EDITING

**Gene editing** is a type of genetic engineering that is even more precise than genetic modification. One form of gene editing, known as CRISPR technology, gives scientists the ability to cut and edit pieces of DNA at a specific location. This fascinating technology shows great promise in the treatment of genetic disorders, such as sickle cell disease, muscular dystrophy, and cystic fibrosis.

Besides genetic disorders, gene editing could be used to treat and prevent many other health problems. It could be used to treat cancer by targeting specific genes in cancer cells. It could also help prevent infections, such as malaria, which is spread from mosquitoes to humans. Scientists could edit the mosquitoes' DNA to make them resistant to malaria. Additionally, we could use gene editing to help solve our shortage of human organs for donation. Scientists could treat pigs with gene editing to make their organs suitable for transplant in humans.

# DESIGN YOUR BABY

### EYE COLOR

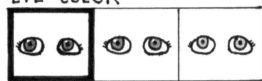

### HAIR COLOR

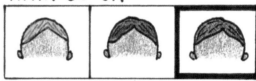

### HANDEDNESS

### HEIGHT

### INTELLIGENCE

### ATHLETIC ABILITY

Even though gene editing has the potential to treat or even cure problems that affect millions of people, it could be harmful to society if used inappropriately. Many people fear that gene editing will give people the power to create "designer babies," allowing parents to choose the traits they want in their children, such as eye color, intelligence, and athletic ability. Also, gene editing is not perfect, and changing someone's DNA could result in unexpected errors. Currently, scientists are in the process of improving this technology, while government authorities are proposing how to best regulate its use.

**Do you think parents in the future should be allowed to use gene editing to choose the genetic traits in their children?**

# THE FUTURE OF GENETICS

Genetics is a very exciting field of research, and new discoveries are being made every day. Innovations in gene testing, genetic engineering, and gene editing are transforming science and medicine and will continue to change society. Learning about the foundations of genetics helps us to better understand these new advancements and allows us to think about new ways to use genetics.

# DISCUSSION QUESTIONS

1. Besides the genetic disorders discussed in this book, name or research another genetic disorder that can be passed on from parents to their children.

2. What are the three main types of mutations? What occurs when a mutation is beneficial?

3. Cystic fibrosis is an autosomal recessive disease. If a father is a carrier for the mutation (Aa) and the mother does not have the mutation (AA), what are the chances that their child will have cystic fibrosis? What are the chances that their child will be a carrier? Draw a Punnett Square to help you.

# DISCUSSION QUESTIONS

4. Do you have a favorite fruit? Would you eat it if you knew it had been genetically modified to be bigger, sweeter, and always perfectly ripe? What if you were told it was safe?

5. What could happen if gene editing was not regulated and anyone could use this technology for their own benefit?

6. If available to you in the future, would you want to have your entire personal genome tested? What would be the benefits of having this information? What would be the disadvantages?

# GLOSSARY

**Allele** - one member of a pair of genes that is located on a specific location on a chromosome

**Ancestry** - a person's ethnic origin or descent; where one's ancestors came from

**Autosomal dominant disorder** - a genetic disorder in which only one abnormal gene from one parent is needed to get the disease

**Autosomal recessive disorder** - a genetic disorder in which two copies of an abnormal gene, one from each parent, must be present in order to get the disease

**Carrier** - a person or other organism that has inherited a recessive allele for a genetic trait or mutation but does not display that trait or show symptoms of the disease

**Cell** - the smallest unit of living organisms that include all of the properties of life

**Chromosome** - a structure found within the nucleus of a cell that holds the genetic material of DNA

**Deletion** - a type of mutation that occurs when a base is taken out of the gene sequence

**DNA** - a double stranded nucleic acid arranged as a double helix that is part of a chromosome and contains genes

**Evolution** - the process of gradual change that takes place over many generations, during which some of the traits of species slowly change

**Gene** - the basic unit of heredity that is located on a specific location of DNA

**Gene editing** - the technology used to cut and edit DNA at a specific site

**Gene testing** - the use of laboratory tests to diagnose a genetic disease, evaluate risk for a disease, or determine one's ancestry

**Genetic engineering** - the use of technology to modify the genetic makeup of an organism

**Genetic disorders** - conditions produced by an abnormality in DNA, such as a change in a chromosome or a mutation in a single gene

**Genetically modified organisms** - plants, animals, or microorganisms that have had their DNA changed through genetic engineering

# GLOSSARY

**Genetics** - the study of heredity, genes, and the diversity of organisms

**Genome** - all of the DNA needed to build and maintain that organism

**Genotype** - the genetic makeup of an individual organism

**Heterozygous** - possessing two alleles at a specific gene that are different

**Homozygous** - possessing two alleles at a specific gene that are the same

**Human Genome Project** - international researchers worked together to decipher the entire human genome by determining the order of all of the bases in our DNA

**Inheritance** - the passing on of traits genetically from one generation to the next

**Insertion** - a type of mutation that occurs when an extra base is inserted into the gene sequence

**Karyotype** - a diagram of the number and appearance of chromosomes in the nucleus of a cell

**Mendelian inheritance** - the rules by which genes and traits are passed from parents to children

**Nucleus** - the organelle in a cell that is enclosed in a membrane and contains the chromosomes and genetic material

**Phenotype** - the observable characteristics of an individual organism resulting from the expression of the genotype

**Punnett square** - a square diagram used to predict the probability of offspring genotypes when breeding two organisms

**Substitution** - a type of mutation that occurs when an original base is replaced by a different base

**Trait** - a characteristic or quality that is genetic and inherited

**X-linked disorder** - a genetic disorder caused by a mutation on the X chromosome

**Y-linked disorder** - a genetic disorder caused by a mutation on the Y chromosome

# ABOUT THE AUTHOR

Jane Zebrack is a high school student at Bishop Manogue Catholic High School in Reno, Nevada. Jane has always been fascinated with the study of genetics and how current and future use of gene editing can help those affected by medical conditions. Through *An Introduction to Genetics for Kids*, Jane wishes to raise awareness of genetic diseases and instill in children a passion for learning about genetics and science.

Printed in Great Britain
by Amazon

38728527R00022